2.80

# ELEMENTARY GRAMMAR WORKBOOK 1

MURIEL HIGGINS

TIA M. CARROLL
62 BRIGHTON RD.
COULSDON
SURREY 081-668-3048

Longman

Illustrated by John Millington
and Technical Art Services

**Longman Group UK Limited,**
*Longman House, Burnt Mill, Harlow,*
*Essex CM20 2JE, England*
*and Associated Companies throughout the world.*

© Longman Group Limited 1983
*All rights reserved; no part of this publication may be reproduced, stored in a retrieval system or transmitted in any form or by any means, electronic, mechanical, photocopying, recording, or otherwise, without the prior written permission of the Publishers.*

First published 1983
Seventeenth impression 1991

Set in 10/12pt Linotron 202 Palatino

Produced by Longman Singapore Publishers Pte Ltd.
Printed in Singapore

ISBN 0-582-55890-5

# CONTENTS

# BE

| Anna | Tony | John | Fran | Marie | Pierre |
|---|---|---|---|---|---|
| student | teacher | student | teacher | student | teacher |
| English | English | American | American | French | French |
| London | London | New York | New York | Paris | Paris |

## 1 Write *is* or *are*

| Anna | is | a student. |
|---|---|---|
| John and Marie | are | students. |

| Anna | is | English. |
|---|---|---|
| John and Fran | are | American. |

1 Anna *is* a student.
2 Pierre ______ a teacher.
3 Marie and John ______ students.
4 Tony ______ a teacher.
5 Fran ______ a teacher.
6 Tony and Fran ______ teachers.
7 Anna *is* English.
8 Fran ______ American.
9 Pierre and Marie ______ French.
10 Tony and Anna ______ English.
11 John and Fran ______ American.
12 Tony ______ English.

## 2 Ask and answer

| Is | Anna | a teacher? |
|---|---|---|
| Are | Fran and Tony | teachers? |

| Yes./No. |
|---|

1 Anna/a teacher
*Is Anna a teacher? No.*
2 John and Marie/students
______
3 Fran/a teacher
______
4 Pierre and Tony/teachers
______
5 Anna/a student
______
6 Fran and Tony/students
______

## 3 Write *is/isn't/are/aren't*

| John | is<br>isn't | English.<br>American.<br>French. |
|---|---|---|
| Anna and Tony | are<br>aren't | |

1 John *isn't* English. He *is* American.
2 Anna *is* English. She *isn't* American.
3 Marie and Pierre ______ French. They ______ English.
4 Anna ______ American. She ______ English.
5 Fran and John ______ American. They ______ English.
6 Pierre ______ English. He ______ French.
7 Tony ______ English. He ______ French and he ______ American.

## 4 Ask and answer

| Where | is | Tony?<br>Anna? |
|---|---|---|
| | are | John and Fran? |

| He<br>She | is | in | London.<br>New York.<br>Paris. |
|---|---|---|---|
| They | are | | |

1 Marie
*Where is Marie? She is in Paris.*
2 John and Fran
______________________
3 Tony
______________________
4 Pierre and Marie
______________________

## 5 Who is it?

1

*Marie*

2

______________________

3

______________________

4

______________________

## 6 Find the answer

1 Are you Greek, Anna? *No, I'm English.*
2 Are you a teacher, Marie? ______
3 Are you a student, John? ______
4 Are you French, Tony? ______
5 Are you a student, Pierre? ______
6 Are you a teacher, Fran? ______

ANSWERS

| | | |
|---|---|---|
| No, I'm a student. | Yes, I'm a student. | No, I'm not French. |
| No, I'm English. | No, I'm a teacher. | Yes, I'm a teacher. |

## 7 Write what Anna, John and Pierre say

| I | 'm (am) |
|---|---|
| He She | 's (is) |

| I'm | not |
|---|---|
| He She | isn't |

Anna is English. She isn't American. And she isn't a teacher, she is a student.

ANNA: *I'm English. I'm not American. And I'm not a teacher, I'm a student.*

JOHN: ______

______

PIERRE: ______

______

## 8 What about you? And your friend?

My name is ______ His/Her name is ______
I'm ______ ______ is ______
I'm not ______ ______ isn't ______
I'm a ______ ______ is a ______
I'm not a ______ ______ isn't a ______

# HAVE

| I<br>You<br>We<br>They | have |
|---|---|
| He<br>She | has |

| I<br>You<br>We<br>They | don't have |
|---|---|
| He<br>She | doesn't have |

## 1 Read and write

This is the Green family.

Mr Green is the father. Mrs Green is the mother.
Mr and Mrs Green have four children. They have two boys,

Don and Joe, and two girls, Jenny and Penny.

Don and Joe have two sisters, and Jenny and Penny have two brothers.

**Write *has* or *have* and a number: *1 one/2 two/3 three/4 four***

1 Mr and Mrs Green *have* *four* children.
2 They ______ ______ boys.
3 Don ______ ______ sisters and ______ brother.
4 Jenny and Penny ______ ______ brothers.
5 Joe ______ ______ brother, and he ______ ______ sisters.
6 Penny ______ ______ sister, and she ______ ______ brothers.

## 2 What do they have?

1 The Greens/a dog — *The Greens have a dog.*
2 Mr Green/a car — ______
3 Don/a bicycle — ______
4 Jenny/a radio — ______
5 Penny/a camera — ______
6 The girls/a bird — ______

## 3 What don't they have?

1 Mrs Green/a car *Mrs Green doesn't have a car.*

2 Joe/an umbrella

3 The children/a cat

4 Don/a camera

5 Mr Green/a bird

6 Jenny and Penny/an elephant

## 4 What about you and your family?

| Yes, I/we have a . . . |
|---|
| No, I/we don't have a . . . |

Do you have . . .

. . . a car?

. . . a bicycle?

. . . a dog?

. . . a cat?

. . . a radio?

. . . a television set?

. . . an elephant?

## 5 And what about your friend?

| Yes, he/she has a . . . |
|---|
| No, he/she doesn't have a . . . |

Does your friend have . . .

. . . an umbrella?

. . . a car?

. . . a bicycle?

. . . a television set?

. . . a bird?

## 6 Write sentences

> I have a . . . , but my friend doesn't have a . . . .
> My friend has a . . . , but I don't have a . . . .

I

My friend

I

# ARTICLES: A/AN, THE

## 1 Write *a* or *an*

| a | cat<br>bee<br>parrot |
|---|---|

| an | elephant<br>ant<br>owl |
|---|---|

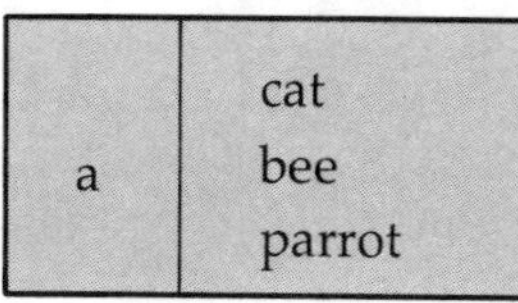

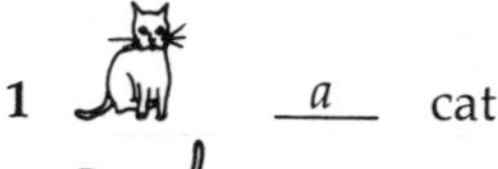

1 *a* cat
2 ___ owl
3 ___ donkey
4 ___ ant
5 ___ dog
6 ___ bee
7 ___ parrot
8 ___ elephant

## 2 Look and write

animals

insects

birds

1 *A* dog *is an animal.*
2 ___ owl ___
3 ___ bee ___
4 ___ donkey ___
5 ___ ant ___
6 ___ elephant ___
7 ___ cat ___
8 ___ parrot ___

## 3 Ask and answer

| Is | a bee<br>an owl | a bird<br>an animal<br>an insect | ? |
|---|---|---|---|

Yes, it is.
No, it isn't.

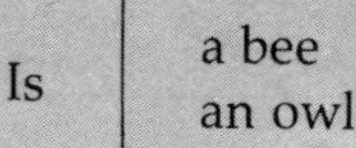

1 bee/insect? *Is a bee an insect?* *Yes, it is.*
2 elephant/bird? *Is an elephant a bird?* *No, it isn't.*
3 owl/bird? ___ ___
4 donkey/animal? ___ ___
5 camel/animal?  ___ ___
6 duck/insect? 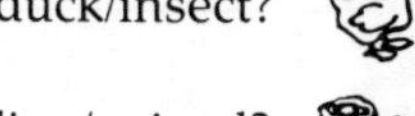 ___ ___
7 lion/animal? 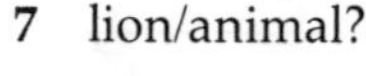 ___ ___
8 eagle/bird? 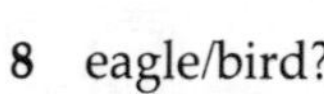 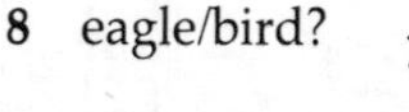 ___ ___
9 octopus/bird? 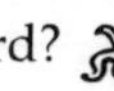  ___ ___

# 4 What are they?

1 Spotty *is an insect.*
2 Shu-shu ______
3 Sam ______
4 Susie ______
5 Snoopy ______
6 Stripy ______

# 5 Look at this

| | |
|---|---|
| 1 A glass, an egg. | 2 The egg is in the glass. |
| 3 A handkerchief. | 4 The handkerchief is over the glass. |
| 5 The handkerchief. | 6 The glass! |
| 7 Where is the egg? | 8 The egg! |

**Now write**

| | | | |
|---|---|---|---|
| 1 *A* *an apple* | 2 ______ ______ | 3 ______ | 4 ______ ______ |
| 5 ______ | 6 ______ | 7 ______ ______ | 8 ______ |

# DEMONSTRATIVES: THIS/THAT/THESE/THOSE

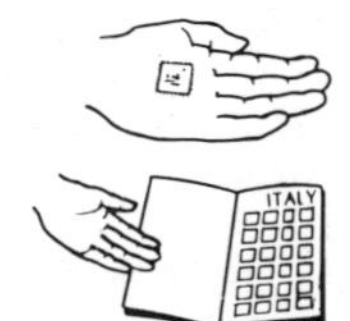

| this stamp<br>these stamps | that stamp<br>those stamps |
|---|---|

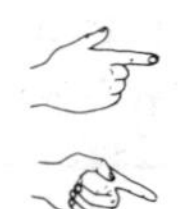
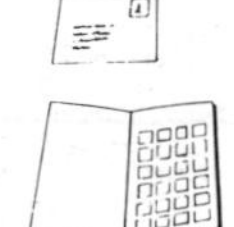

## 1 Write *This* or *That* and finish the sentences

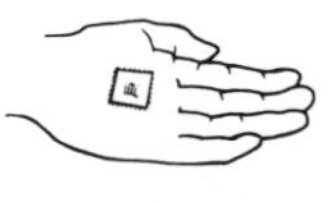

1 *This* stamp *is* Greek.

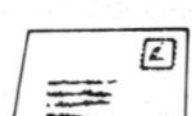

2 *That* stamp *is* Italian.

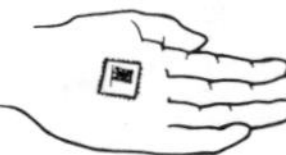

3 ______________________ British.

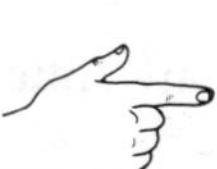
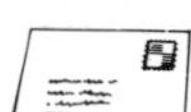

4 ______________________ American.

5 ______________________ French.

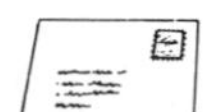

6 ______________________ Greek.

## 2 Write sentences with *These* or *Those*

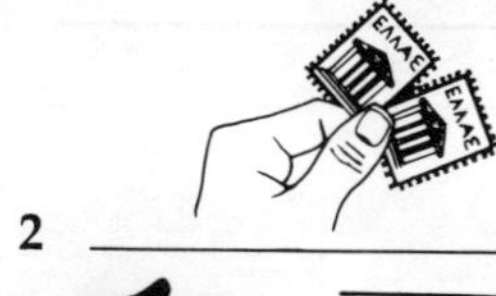

1 *These stamps are Greek.*

2 ______________________

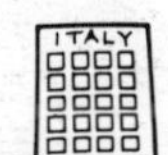

3 ______________________

4 ______________________

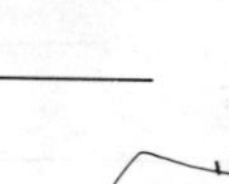

5 ______________________

6 ______________________ , too.

## 3 Find the right answer

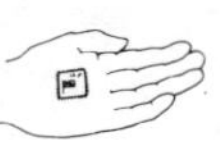

1 | This / ~~That~~ | stamp is Greek.

2 | Those stamps are / That stamp is | British.

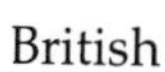

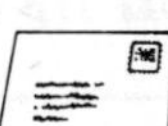

3 | These / Those | stamps are Italian.

4 | This / That | stamp is French.

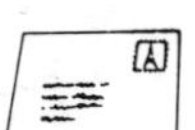

# 4 Finish these sentences

| | | |
|---|---|---|
| This stamp is British. | = | This is a British stamp. |
| That stamp is British. | = | That's a British stamp. |

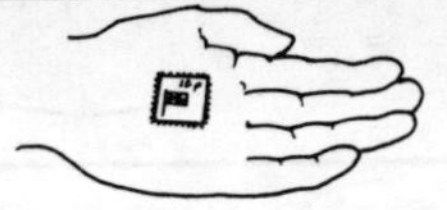

1 *This stamp* is British.
*This* is a British stamp.

2 ________ is a French stamp.
________________ is French.

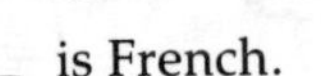

3 ________________ are American.
________ are American stamps.

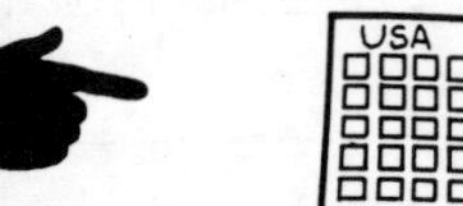

4 ________ are Greek stamps.
________________ are Greek.

5 ________________ is Italian.
________ is an Italian stamp.

# 5 Write two sentences

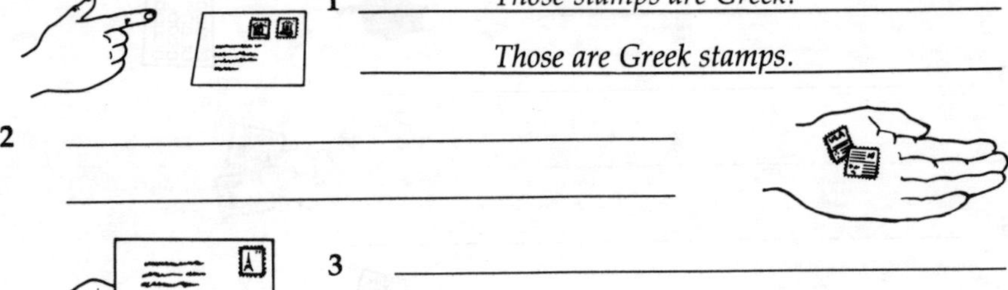

1 *Those stamps are Greek.*
*Those are Greek stamps.*

2 ________________________________
________________________________

3 ________________________________
________________________________

4 ________________________________
________________________________

# 6 Do you have a British stamp?

| Put a British stamp here |
|---|

This stamp ________________________

This is ________________________

# NOUNS

## COUNTABLE NOUNS

### 1 Complete, with these nouns

books boys flowers
pencils radios keys

1 *two pencils* ______

2 ______

3 ______

4 ______

5 ______

6 ______

### 2 Write the plurals of these nouns

actress apple baby camera city country
glass horse lady match stamp watch

| 1 + s | 2 + es | 3 ~~y~~ + ies |
|---|---|---|
| *apples* | *actresses* | *babies* |
| ______ | ______ | ______ |
| ______ | ______ | ______ |
| ______ | ______ | ______ |

### 3 Write and draw

1

a man and a woman

two *men* and two *women*

2

a knife and a fork — two ________ and two forks

3

a sheep — three ________

4

a foot — two ________

5

a baby with one tooth — a baby with two ________

6

a mouse — three ________

7

a fish — four ________

8

a thief — two ________

## UNCOUNTABLE NOUNS

## 4 Complete with *glass/bottle/piece/kilo of . . .*

1 water — a ___*glass of*___ water — ___ jug ________

2 Coca Cola — a ________ — a ________

3 chalk — a ________ — ___ box ________

4 cheese — a ________ — a ________

5 meat — a ________

6 chocolate — a ________ — ___ bar ________

## PROPER NOUNS

### 5 Write true sentences from the table

Cities and countries start with a CAPITAL LETTER

| ATHENS<br>BOSTON<br>LONDON<br>MILAN<br>NEW YORK<br>OXFORD<br>PARIS<br>ROME | IS | A CITY IN<br>THE CAPITAL OF | ENGLAND.<br>FRANCE.<br>GREECE.<br>ITALY.<br>THE UNITED STATES. |
|---|---|---|---|

1 Athens *is the capital of Greece.*
2 Boston ______
3 ______
4 ______
5 ______
6 ______
7 ______
8 ______

### 6 Write these sentences correctly

Days and months start with a CAPITAL LETTER
Names of people and places start with a CAPITAL LETTER

1 IT IS MONDAY MORNING. *It is Monday morning.*
2 IT IS MONDAY THE THIRD OF APRIL. ______
3 MR SMITH IS IN PARIS. ______
4 ANNA ISN'T IN PARIS. ______
5 SHE ISN'T IN FRANCE. ______
6 SHE'S IN ENGLAND. ______
7 SHE'S IN MR BROWN'S OFFICE. ______
8 THE OFFICE IS IN OXFORD STREET. ______
9 MR SMITH IS TELEPHONING. ______
10 'IS THAT YOU, MISS BROWN?' ______
11 'YES, THIS IS ANNA BROWN. ______
12 GOOD MORNING, MR SMITH.' ______

# POSSESSIVES

## 7 Choose the right answer

| | |
|---|---|
| the girl's umbrellas | the girls' umbrellas |
| the girls' umbrella | the girl's umbrella |

1 *the girl's umbrella*

3 ____________

2 ____________

4 ____________

## 8 Look and write

1 John  radio 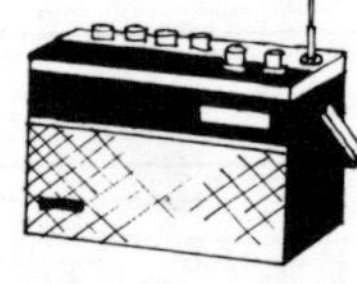 *John's radio*

2 the Greens  dog  ____________

3 Mrs Green  basket  ____________

4 the girls  bird  ____________

5 Mr Green  car  ____________

6 the boys  shirts ____________

7 the family  house  ____________

## 9 Look and write

| living things | 's or s' | Mr Green's car<br>the girls' bedroom<br>the dog's basket |
|---|---|---|
| other things | of the | the windows of the house<br>the side of the house |

**Look at this house**
It's the Greens' house.
It has a living room, a dining room, a kitchen, a bathroom and four bedrooms.

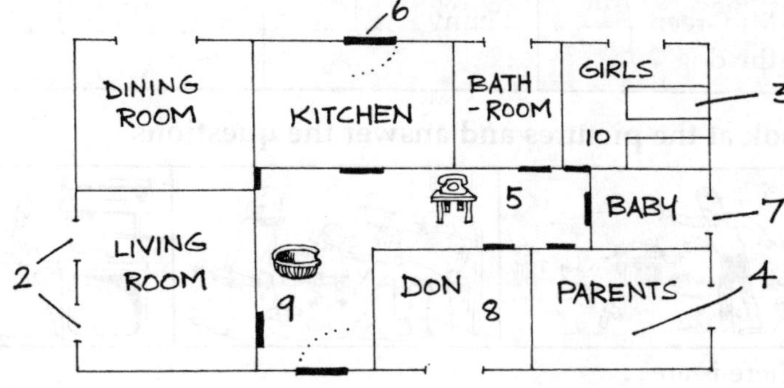


**Look at the plan of the house, and write**

1 house/Greens — *the Greens' house*
2 windows/living room — *the windows of the living room*
3 bed/Jenny — ______
4 bedroom/parents — ______
5 telephone/Greens — ______
6 back door/house — ______
7 window/baby's room — ______
8 Don/bedroom — ______
9 basket/dog — ______
10 door/girls' room — ______

## 0 Write sentences

1 Don/bedroom/at/front/house

*Don's bedroom is at the front of the house.*

2 windows/living room/at/side/house

______

3 bathroom/at/back/house

______

4 baby/room/at/side/house

______

# PRONOUNS

## 1 SUBJECT PRONOUNS

| | | | | | | | |
|---|---|---|---|---|---|---|---|
| Don<br>the baby<br>Mr Green<br>the dog | he | Mrs Green<br>Jenny<br>Penny | she | the house<br>the garden<br>the radio | it | Mr and Mrs Green<br>Jenny and Penny<br>the TV and the radio | they |

**Look at the pictures and answer the questions**

Where is/are . . .

1 . . . Mr Green? *He is in the garden.*

2 . . . Jenny and Penny? *They are in the bedroom.*

3 . . . Mrs Green? ______

4 . . . Don? ______

5 . . . the baby? ______

6 . . . Mr Green and the dog? ______

## 2 SUBJECT AND OBJECT PRONOUNS

| SUBJECT | OBJECT AND AFTER PREPOSITION |
|---|---|
| I | me |
| you | you |
| he | him |
| she | her |
| it | it |
| we | us |
| they | them |

**Answer these questions**

Where can you see . . .

1 . . . Jenny? *I can see her in the bedroom.*

2 . . . Mrs Green? ______

3 . . . Don? ______

4 . . . the girls? ______

5 . . . Mr Green and the dog? ______

6 . . . the radio? ______

7 . . . the baby? ______

8 . . . Penny? ______

# 3 What do they say?

| | |
|---|---|
| MRS GREEN: | It's lunch time! Don! Girls! Where are you? |
| DON: | [1] *I'm* in the [2] *living room*. |
| MRS GREEN: | What about the girls? Are [3] ______ with [4] ______? |
| DON: | No, [5] ______ aren't [6] ______ me. |
| JENNY AND PENNY: | [7] ______ in the bedroom. |
| MRS GREEN: | It's lunch time. Where's Dad? |
| JENNY: | [8] ______ in the [9] ______. I can see [10] ______. Dad! |
| MRS GREEN: | Lunch! Are you there, Bob? Jenny! Penny! |
| MR GREEN: | OK, [11] ______ in the dining room. |
| JENNY AND PENNY: | And [12] ______ in the dining room, too, now. |
| MRS GREEN: | Where's Don? Is [13] ______ with [14] ______? |
| PENNY: | No, [15] ______ in the living room. He's watching TV. |
| MRS GREEN: | Don! Don!! |

# 4 POSSESSIVES

| | | | |
|---|---|---|---|
| (I) | my | (we) | our |
| (you) | your | (they) | their |
| (he) | his | | |
| (she) | her | | |
| (it) | its | | |

### Write questions and answers

1 Penny/camera — *Does Penny have a camera?*
*Yes, that's her camera.*

2 the Greens/garden ______________________
______________________

3 Don/football ______________________
______________________

4 the children/dog ______________________
______________________

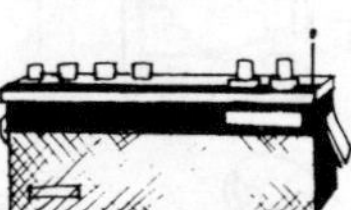

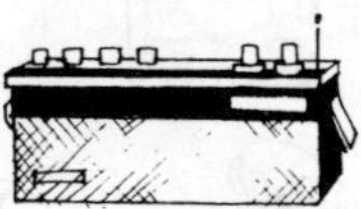

5 Mrs Green/radio ______________________
______________________

6 Mr Green/car ______________________
______________________

# 5 What about you and your family?

**Draw and write sentences**

I have *a* ______________________

This is *my* ______________________

My friend has ______________________

This ______________________

At home we ______________________

This ______________________

# 6 *Your* or *you're*? *Its* or *it's*? *Their* or *they're*?

| POSSESSIVE | PRONOUN + VERB |
|---|---|
| your<br>its<br>their | you're (= you are)<br>it's (= it is)<br>they're (= they are) |

**Write *your* or *you're***

**A** This is [1] *your* book. [2] *You're* reading it. It's [3] ______ English book. [4] ______ learning English. [5] ______________ reading [6] ______ English book.

**Write *its* or *it's***

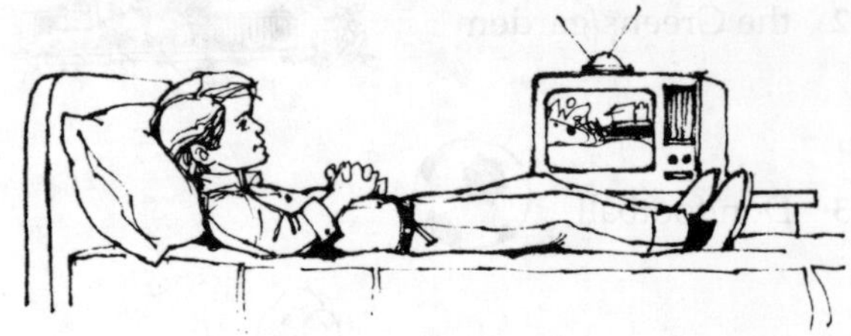

**B** John has a television set in his bedroom. [1] ______ small, but [2] ______ picture is very good. [3] ______ German. It has an aerial. Can you see [4] ______ aerial?

**Write *their* or *they're***

**C** Can you see the girls?

[1] ________ in [2] ____________ bedroom. [3] ______ names are Jenny and Penny. Mrs Green says 'Jenny, Penny!' It's lunch time and [4] ________ lunch is ready. [5] ________ in the dining room now.

# PRESENT PROGRESSIVE

## 1 What are they doing?

**Look at the pictures and write six sentences**

| The baby<br>Penny<br>The dog<br>Don | is | washing the car.<br>feeding the baby.<br>eating.<br>playing tennis.<br>sleeping.<br>working in the garden. |
|---|---|---|
| Jenny and her friend<br>Mr and Mrs Green | are | |

1 *The baby is eating.*
2 ______
3 ______
4 ______
5 ______
6 ______

## 2 Correct these sentences

| No, | he<br>she | isn't | . . . ing . . . |
|---|---|---|---|
| | they | aren't | |

1 Penny is feeding the dog.

*No, she isn't feeding the dog. She's feeding the baby.*

2 Don is washing the windows.

______

3 Jenny and her friend are playing football.

______

4 The baby is sleeping.

______

5 Mr and Mrs Green are working in the kitchen.

______

6 The dog is eating.

______

## 3 Who? What? Where?

**Look at the answers and write the questions**

1 *Where are* Mr and Mrs Green working? — In the garden.

2 *What is* Jenny doing? — Playing tennis.

3 ____________ feeding the baby? — Penny.

4 ____________ the baby eating? — In the kitchen.

5 ____________ Don washing? — The car.

6 ____________ he washing it? — In the garden.

7 ____________ Mr and Mrs Green doing? — Digging.

## 4 Ask and answer

| | | |
|---|---|---|
| Is | the baby<br>Don<br>Penny | sleeping?<br>working?<br>eating?<br>working in the garden? |
| Are | Mr and Mrs Green | |

| | | |
|---|---|---|
| Yes, | he<br>she | is. |
| | they are. | |
| No, | he<br>she | isn't. |
| | they aren't. | |

1 baby/sleeping

*Is the baby sleeping?* ____________ *No, he isn't.*

2 girls/doing their homework

____________ ____________

3 Don/watching football on TV

____________ ____________

4 Mr Green/working

____________ ____________

5 he/working/in his office

____________ ____________

6 Penny and the baby/playing

____________ ____________

## 5 What about you? What are you doing now? And where?

I'm ____________

# THERE IS/THERE ARE; PREPOSITIONS (PLACE)

| There | is<br>isn't | (SINGULAR) |
|---|---|---|

| There | are<br>aren't | (PLURAL) |
|---|---|---|

## 1 Look and write *There is* or *There are*

This is a room in a big hotel.

1 *There are* two beds.
2 ______ a bathroom.
3 ______ a television.
4 ______ four chairs.
5 ______ a telephone.
6 ______ two mirrors.
7 ______ three tables.
8 ______ a picture on the wall.

## 2 Write sentences about this room in a small hotel

1 a bathroom
*There isn't a bathroom.*

2 a television
______

3 a telephone
______

4 a picture on the wall
______

5 two beds
*There aren't two beds. There is one bed.*

6 four chairs
______

7 two mirrors
______

8 three tables
______

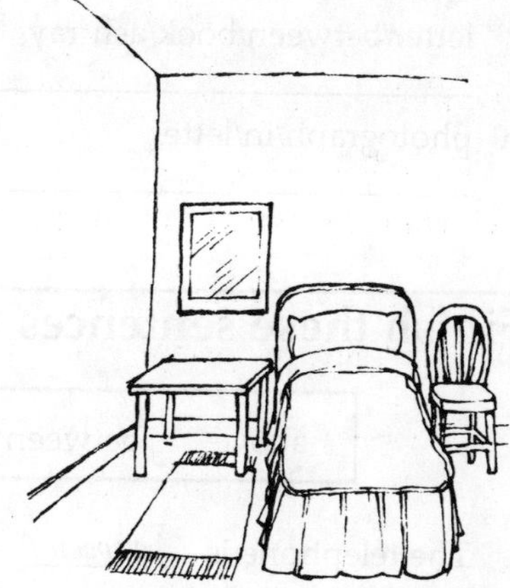

## 3 What about your room?

In my room there is ______. There is ______, too. But there isn't ______, and there isn't ______. There are ______ and ______
______

# 4 Write sentences about this room in the big hotel

1 light/above/bed

*There's a light above the bed.*

2 small table/beside/bed

3 telephone/on/small table

4 mirror/above/large table

5 bag/under/table

6 chair/in front of/table

7 book/on/table

8 ashtray/on/table

9 letter/between/book/ashtray

10 photograph/in/letter

# 5 Finish these sentences with these prepositions

| above | between | beside | in | near | on | under |
|---|---|---|---|---|---|---|

1 The telephone is *between* the bed and the table.

2 The bag is ______ the chair.

3 The photograph is ______ the letter.

4 The mirror is ______ the table.

5 The bag is ______ the table.

6 The book is ______ the table.

7 There's a small table ______ the bed and the large table.

## 6 Write questions with *Is there . . .?* or *Are there . . .?*

1 a post office *Is there a post office near the hotel?*
2 museums ______
3 a bus stop ______
4 theatres ______
5 cinemas ______
6 a bookshop ______

## 7 What about your home? Give short answers

Yes, there is/are.
No, there isn't/aren't.

Is there a post office near your house? ______
Is there a museum? ______
Is there a bus stop near your home? ______
Is there a cinema? ______
Is there a school near your house? ______
Are there a lot of shops? ______
Are there a lot of trees near your home? ______

## 8 Finish the conversation with *there* or *it*

Jim is asking Nick about hotels in a big city.

JIM: Is [1]*there* a snack-bar at the Dolphin Hotel?
NICK: Yes, and [2]*it*'s a very good snack-bar.
JIM: Is [3]______ a restaurant?
NICK: Yes, [4]______ is.
JIM: What about the swimming pool? Is [5]______ big?
NICK: No, [6]______ isn't. But [7]______ 's a big pool at the Grand Hotel.
JIM: And tell me about the restaurant at the Grand. Is [8]______ good?
NICK: Yes, very good. In fact [9]______ are two restaurants.
JIM: Two? Is [10]______ a very big hotel, then?
NICK: Well, yes, [11]______ is, it has 300 rooms.
JIM: Is [12]______ very busy in summer?
NICK: Of course. [13]______ are a lot of tourists here then.

# SOME/ANY

## 1

| IN AFFIRMATIVE STATEMENTS | | | |
|---|---|---|---|
| *some* + uncountable noun | | *some* + plural noun | |
| some | fruit<br>milk | some | apples<br>tomatoes |

**Write sentences**

What is there in the refrigerator?

1 Fruit? Yes, *there's some fruit.*

2 Apples? Yes, *there are some apples.*

3 Milk? Yes, ____________________

4 Butter? Yes, ____________________

5 Vegetables? Yes, ____________________

6 Tomatoes? Yes, ____________________

7 Meat? Yes, ____________________

## 2

| IN QUESTIONS AND NEGATIVE STATEMENTS | | | | | |
|---|---|---|---|---|---|
| *any* + uncountable noun | | | *any* + plural noun | | |
| (not) | any | cheese<br>wine | (not) | any | grapes<br>eggs |

**Answer the questions**

Is/Are there any . . .

1 . . . cheese? No, *there isn't any cheese.*

2 . . . eggs? No, *there aren't any eggs.*

3 . . . milk? Yes, ____________________

4 . . . potatoes? No, ____________________

5 . . . tomatoes? Yes, ____________________

6 . . . wine? No, ____________________

7 . . . lemons? No, ____________________

## 3 Ask questions and answer

1 bread *Is there any bread?*  *No, there isn't.*

2 ice ______ ✓ ______

3 beans ______ ✗ ______

4 jam ______ ✓ ______

5 pears ______ ✓ ______

6 grapes ______ ✗ ______

## 4 What about your kitchen? Write about it

There's some ______, and there's some ______

There are ______

There isn't any ______, and there isn't ______

There aren't ______

______

## 5 Look

Andrew, Betty, Dot and Fred are eating.
There's some cheese, some eggs,
some salad and some fruit.
Who has what?

| | cheese | eggs | salad | fruit |
|---|---|---|---|---|
| Andrew | ✓ | ✗ | ✓ | ✓ |
| Betty | ✓ | ✓ | ✓ | ✗ |
| Dot | ✓ | ✓ | ✗ | ✓ |
| Fred | ✗ | ✓ | ✓ | ✗ |

**Write sentences and draw pictures**

1 Andrew *has some cheese, some salad and some fruit*, but *he doesn't have any eggs.*

Andrew's lunch

Betty's lunch

2 Betty ______
______, but
______

3 Dot ______
______, but
______

Fred's lunch

Dot's lunch

4 Fred ______
______, but
______

## 6 Read and then write the conversations

Maria is buying some fruit.

| | |
|---|---|
| MARIA: | Do you have any bananas? |
| WOMAN: | No, I'm sorry, there aren't any bananas today. |
| MARIA: | Well, do you have any grapes, please? |
| WOMAN: | No, I don't have any grapes, either. |
| MARIA: | Do you have any apples, then? |
| WOMAN: | Yes, I have some very nice apples. |

**1** You are buying vegetables. (beans ✗, tomatoes ✗ and potatoes ✓)

YOU: ______

MAN: ______

YOU: ______

MAN: ______

YOU: ______

MAN: ______

______

**2** You want some ice cream. (chocolate ice cream ✗, coffee ice cream ✗ and lemon ice cream ✓.)

YOU: ______

MAN: ______

YOU: ______

MAN: ______

YOU: ______

MAN: ______

**3** You want some flowers for your friend in hospital. (red roses ✗, yellow roses ✗, white roses ✓.)

YOU: ______

WOMAN: ______

YOU: ______

WOMAN: ______

YOU: ______

WOMAN: ______

# HOW MUCH? HOW MANY?

| HOW MUCH + UNCOUNTABLE | | | HOW MANY + PLURAL | | |
|---|---|---|---|---|---|
| How much | sugar<br>butter | . . .? | How many | eggs<br>apples | . . .? |

## 1 Read and then write conversations

You're making a cake with your friend, Jan.

| | |
|---|---|
| YOU: | How much flour is there in the cake? |
| JAN: | 500 gms. |
| YOU: | How much flour do we have? |
| JAN: | Oh dear, only 250 gms. |

**1** (sugar)

YOU: *How much sugar is there in the cake?*

JAN: 250 gms.

YOU: ______________________

JAN: Only 100 gms.

**2** (butter)

YOU: ______________________

JAN: 350 gms.

YOU: ______________________

JAN: Oh. Only 250 gms.

**3** (eggs)

YOU: ______________________

JAN: Four.

YOU: ______________________

JAN: Oh dear, we only have three.

**4** (chocolate)

YOU: ______________________

JAN: 100 gms.

YOU: ______________________

JAN: We don't have any chocolate.

# NUMBERS AND TIME

## TELEPHONE NUMBERS

### 1 Write these numbers in figures

1 three o eight, five two five one _308 5251_

2 five nine eight, seven eight six one ______

3 o three one, three six two seven ______

4 eight four nine, three four three seven ______

5 six o two, four five nine two ______

### 2 Write these telephone numbers in words

1 Jane _five nine two, o one three seven_

2 Peter ______

3 Aunt Lydia ______

4 Harry and Kate ______

5 John ______

6 Sylvia ______

## YEARS

### 3 When were they born?

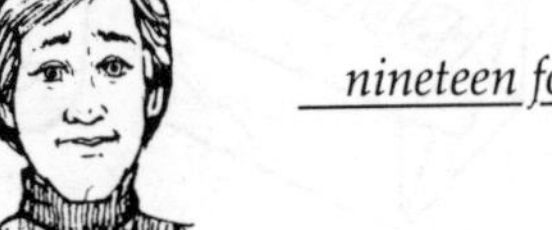

1 1946 _nineteen forty-six_

2 ______ 1898

3 1975 ______

4 ______ 1970

5 1937 ______

6 ______ 1954

# ANSWERS

## BE

**Ex 1** 1 is 2 is 3 are 4 is 5 is 6 are 7 is 8 is 9 are 10 are 11 are 12 is

**Ex 2** 1 Is Anna a teacher? No. 2 Are John and Marie students? Yes. 3 Is Fran a teacher? Yes. 4 Are Pierre and Tony teachers? Yes. 5 Is Anna a student? Yes. 6 Are Fran and Tony students? No.

**Ex 3** 1 isn't, is 2 is, isn't 3 are, aren't 4 isn't, is 5 are, aren't 6 isn't, is 7 is, isn't, isn't

**Ex 4** 1 Where is Marie? She is in Paris. 2 Where are John and Fran? They are in New York. 3 Where is Tony? He is in London. 4 Where are Pierre and Marie? They are in Paris.

**Ex 5** 1 Marie 2 Anna 3 John and Fran 4 Anna and Tony

**Ex 6** 1 No, I'm English. 2 No, I'm a student. 3 Yes, I'm a student. 4 No, I'm not French. 5 No, I'm a teacher. 6 Yes, I'm a teacher.

**Ex 7** 1 I'm English. I'm not American. And I'm not a teacher, I'm a student. 2 I'm American. I'm not English/French. And I'm not a teacher, I'm a student. 3 I'm French. I'm not English/American. And I'm not a student, I'm a teacher.

**Ex 8** (*student's own answers*)

## HAVE

**Ex 1** 1 have four 2 have two 3 has two, one 4 have two 5 has one, has two 6 has one, has two

**Ex 2** 1 The Greens have a dog. 2 Mr Green has a car. 3 Don has a bicycle. 4 Jenny has a radio. 5 Penny has a camera. 6 The girls have a bird.

**Ex 3** 1 Mrs Green doesn't have a car. 2 Joe doesn't have an umbrella. 3 The children don't have a cat. 4 Don doesn't have a camera. 5 Mr Green doesn't have a bird. 6 Jenny and Penny don't have an elephant.

**Ex 4, Ex 5, Ex 6** (*student's own answers*)

## ARTICLES

**Ex 1** 1 a 2 an 3 a 4 an 5 a 6 a 7 a 8 an

**Ex 2** 1 A dog is an animal. 2 An owl is a bird. 3 A bee is an insect. 4 A donkey is an animal. 5 An ant is an insect. 6 An elephant is an animal. 7 A cat is an animal. 8 A parrot is a bird.

**Ex 3** 1 Is a bee an insect? Yes, it is. 2 Is an elephant a bird? No, it isn't. 3 Is an owl a bird? Yes, it is. 4 Is a donkey an animal? Yes, it is. 5 Is a camel an animal? Yes, it is. 6 Is a duck an insect? No, it isn't. 7 Is a lion an animal? Yes, it is. 8 Is an eagle a bird? Yes, it is. 9 Is an octopus a bird? No, it isn't.

**Ex 4** 1 is an insect. 2 is an animal. 3 is a bird. 4 is an animal. 5 is an animal. 6 is an animal.

**Ex 5** 1 a glass, an apple 2 The apple is in the glass. 3 a handkerchief 4 The handkerchief is over the glass. 5 the handkerchief 6 the glass! 7 Where is the apple? 8 The apple!

## DEMONSTRATIVES

**Ex 1** 1 This stamp is 2 That stamp is 3 This stamp is 4 That stamp is 5 This stamp is 6 That stamp is

**Ex 2** 1 These stamps are Greek. 2 Those stamps are Italian. 3 Those stamps are British. 4 These stamps are French. 5 Those stamps are American. 6 These stamps are American, too.

**Ex 3** 1 This 2 That 3 These 4 That

**Ex 4** 1 This stamp, This 2 That, That stamp 3 Those stamps, Those 4 These, These stamps 5 This stamp, This

**Ex 5** 1 Those stamps are Greek. Those are Greek stamps. 2 These stamps are American. These are American stamps. 3 This stamp is French. This is a French stamp. 4 That stamp is British. That is a British stamp.

**Ex 6** 1 is British. a British stamp.

## NOUNS

**Ex 1** 1 two pencils 2 three keys 3 two flowers 4 three radios 5 five books 6 three boys

**Ex 2** 1 apples cameras horses stamps 2 actresses glasses matches watches 3 babies cities countries ladies

**Ex 3** 1 two men and two women 2 two knives and two forks 3 three sheep 4 two feet 5 a baby with two teeth 6 three mice 7 four fish 8 two thieves.

**Ex 4** 1 a glass of water, a jug of water 2 a bottle of Coca Cola, a glass of Coca Cola 3 a piece of chalk, a box of chalk 4 a piece of cheese, a kilo of cheese 5 a piece of meat 6 a piece of chocolate, a bar of chocolate.

**Ex 5** 1 Athens is the capital of Greece. 2 Boston is a city in the United States. 3 London is the capital of England. 4 Milan is a city in Italy. 5 New York is a city in the United States. 6 Oxford is a city in England. 7 Paris is the capital of France. 8 Rome is the capital of Italy.

**Ex 6** 1 It is Monday morning. 2 It is Monday the third of April. 3 Mr Smith is in Paris. 4 Anna isn't in Paris. 5 She isn't in France. 6 She's in England. 7 She's in Mr Brown's office. 8 The office is in Oxford Street. 9 Mr Smith is telephoning. 10 'Is that you, Miss Brown?' 11 'Yes, this is Anna Brown. 12 Good morning, Mr Smith.'

**Ex 7** 1 the girl's umbrella 2 the girls' umbrella 3 the girls' umbrellas 4 the girl's umbrellas

**Ex 8** 1 John's radio 2 the Greens' dog 3 Mrs Green's basket 4 the girls' bird 5 Mr Green's car 6 the boys' shirts 7 the family's house

**Ex 9** 1 the Greens' house 2 the windows of the living room 3 Jenny's bed 4 the parents' bedroom 5 the Greens' telephone 6 the back door of the house 7 the window of the baby's room 8 Don's bedroom 9 the dog's basket 10 the door of the girls' room

**Ex 10** 1 Don's bedroom is at the front of the house. 2 The windows of the living room are at the side of the house. 3 The bathroom is at the back of the house. 4 The baby's room is at the side of the house.

## PRONOUNS

**Ex 1** 1 He is in the garden. 2 They are in the bedroom. 3 She is in the kitchen. 4 He is in the living room. 5 He is in the kitchen. 6 They are in the garden.

**Ex 2** I can see + 1 her in the bedroom. 2 her in the kitchen. 3 him in the living room. 4 them in the bedroom. 5 them in the garden. 6 it in the kitchen. 7 him in the kitchen. 8 her in the bedroom.

**Ex 3** 1 I'm 2 living room 3 they 4 you 5 they 6 with 7 We're 8 He's 9 garden 10 him 11 I'm 12 we're 13 he 14 you 15 he's

**Ex 4** 1 Does Penny have a camera? Yes, that's her camera. 2 Do the Greens have a garden? Yes, that's their garden. 3 Does Don have a football? Yes, that's his football. 4 Do the children have a dog? Yes, that's their dog. 5 Does Mrs Green have a radio? Yes, that's her radio. 6 Does Mr Green have a car? Yes, that's his car.

**Ex 5** (*student's own answers*)

**Ex 6** A1 your 2 You're 3 your 4 You're 5 You're 6 your
B1 It's 2 its 3 It's 4 its
C1 They're 2 their 3 Their 4 their 5 They're

## PRESENT PROGRESSIVE

**Ex 1** 1 The baby is eating. 2 Penny is feeding the baby. 3 The dog is sleeping. 4 Don is washing the car. 5 Jenny and her friend are playing tennis. 6 Mr and Mrs Green are working in the garden.

**Ex 2** 1 No, she isn't feeding the dog. She's feeding the baby. 2 No, he isn't washing the windows. He's washing the car. 3 No, they aren't playing football. They're playing tennis. 4 No, he isn't sleeping. He's eating. 5 No, they aren't working in the kitchen. They're working in the garden. 6 No, he isn't eating. He's sleeping.

**Ex 3** 1 Where are 2 What is 3 Who is 4 Where is 5 What is 6 Where is 7 What are

**Ex 4** 1 Is the baby sleeping? No, he isn't. 2 Are the girls doing their homework? No, they aren't. 3 Is Don watching football on TV? Yes, he is. 4 Is Mr Green working? Yes, he is. 5 Is he working in his office? No, he isn't. 6 Are Penny and the baby playing? No, they aren't.

**Ex 5** (*student's own answers*)

## THERE IS/THERE ARE; PREPOSITIONS (PLACE)

**Ex 1** 1 There are 2 There is 3 There is 4 There are 5 There is 6 There are 7 There are 8 There is

**Ex 2** 1 There isn't a bathroom. 2 There isn't a television. 3 There isn't a telephone. 4 There isn't a picture on the wall. 5 There aren't two beds. There is one bed. 6 There aren't four chairs. There is one chair. 7 There aren't two mirrors. There is one mirror. 8 There aren't three tables. There is one table.

**Ex 3** (*student's own answers*)

**Ex 4** 1 There's a light above the bed. 2 There's a small table beside the bed. 3 There's a telephone on the small table. 4 There's a mirror above the large table. 5 There's a bag under the table. 6 There's a chair in front of the table. 7 There's a book on the table. 8 There's an ashtray on the table. 9 There's a letter between the book and the ashtray. 10 There's a photograph in the letter.

**Ex 5** 1 between 2 near/beside 3 in 4 above 5 under 6 on 7 between

**Ex 6** 1 Is there a post office near the hotel? 2 Are there museums near the hotel? 3 Is there a bus stop near the hotel? 4 Are there theatres near the hotel? 5 Are there cinemas near the hotel? 6 Is there a bookshop near the hotel?

**Ex 7** (*student's own answers*)

**Ex 8** 1 there 2 it 3 there 4 there 5 it 6 it 7 there 8 it 9 there 10 it 11 it 12 it 13 There

## SOME/ANY

**Ex 1** 1 there's some fruit. 2 there are some apples. 3 there's some milk. 4 there's some butter. 5 there are some vegetables. 6 there are some tomatoes. 7 there's some meat.

**Ex 2** 1 there isn't any cheese. 2 there aren't any eggs. 3 there is some milk. 4 there aren't any potatoes. 5 there are some tomatoes. 6 there isn't any wine. 7 there aren't any lemons.

**Ex 3** 1 Is there any bread? No, there isn't. 2 Is there any ice? Yes, there is. 3 Are there any beans? No, there aren't. 4 Is there any jam? Yes, there is. 5 Are there any pears? Yes, there are. 6 Are there any grapes? No, there aren't.

**Ex 4** (*student's own answers*)

**Ex 5** 1 Andrew has some cheese, some salad and some fruit, but he doesn't have any eggs. 2 Betty has some cheese, some eggs and some salad, but she doesn't have any fruit. 3 Dot has some cheese, some eggs and some fruit, but she doesn't have any salad. 4 Fred has some eggs, some salad and some fruit, but he doesn't have any cheese.

**Ex 6** (*answers follow model dialogue*)

## HOW MUCH? HOW MANY?

**Ex 1** 1 How much sugar is there in the cake? How much sugar do we have? 2 How much butter is there in the cake? How much butter do we have? 3 How many eggs are there in the cake? How many eggs do we have? 4 How much chocolate is there in the cake? How much chocolate do we have?

## NUMBERS AND TIME

**Ex 1** 1 308 5251 2 598 7861 3 031 3627 4 849 3437 5 602 4592

**Ex 2** 1 five nine two, o one three seven 2 eight seven nine, two five two nine 3 six two six, seven five three eight 4 two six seven, three one four six 5 three eight seven, nine four o two 6 four eight six, o six five nine

**Ex 3** 1 nineteen forty-six 2 eighteen ninety-eight 3 nineteen seventy-five 4 nineteen seventy 5 nineteen thirty-seven 6 nineteen fifty-four

**Ex 4** 1 3187 2 2232 3 352 4 9468 5 1541 6 669 7 4773 8 twenty-two thousand two hundred and twenty-two

**Ex 5** 1 eighty, eighteen 2 fifteen, fifty 3 forty, fourteen 4 seventy, seventeen 5 thirty, thirteen 6 sixteen, sixty

**Ex 6** 1 ✓ 2 x 3 ✓ 4 x 5 ✓ 6 x 7 ✓ 8 ✓ 9 ✓

**Ex 7** 1 first 2 second 3 fourth 4 eighth 5 twelfth 6 fifteenth 7 eighteenth 8 twenty-second 9 twenty-sixth (+ is the . . . letter.)

**Ex 8** 1 twelve 2 first 3 twelfth 4 seven 5 thirty 6 second 7 fifty-two 8 seven

**Ex 9** 1 ten o'clock 2 half past two 3 ten to four 4 (a) quarter past one 5 (a) quarter to eleven 6 twenty past six 7 five past nine 8 six o'clock.

**Ex 10** 1 one fifteen 2 seven thirty 3 four ten 4 eleven fourteen 5 three forty 6 eight fifty-five 7 twelve thirty 8 six thirty-eight

## PREPOSITIONS WITH TIME PHRASES

**Ex 1** 1 at 2 in 3 at 4 at 5 in 6 on 7 on 8 in 9 in 10 at

**Ex 2** (*student's own answers*)

## CAN

**Ex 1** (*true answers from table*)

**Ex 2** (*student's own answers*)

**Ex 3** 1 They can climb this tree, but they can't climb that one. 2 He can carry this boat, but he can't carry that one. 3 She can ride this bicycle, but she can't ride that one. 4 He can clean this window, but he can't clean that one. 5 I can post this letter, but I can't post that one. 6 He can carry this case, but he can't carry that one.

**Ex 4** 1 Can Don take good photographs? No, he can't. 2 Can the baby drive the car? No, he can't. 3 Can the girls play tennis? Yes, they can. 4 Can they play football? No, they can't. 5 Can Mr Green cook? Yes, he can.

**Ex 5** 1 Can I borrow your book? 2 Can we watch television? 3 Can I play football? 4 Can I have a new dress? 5 Can we go to the cinema? 6 Can we have a picnic?

**Ex 6** 1 You can, You can't 2 You can't, You can 3 You can't, You can 4 You can't, You can

**Ex 7, Ex 8** (*student's own answers*)

## MUST

**Ex 1** 1 You must turn right. 2 You must be careful. 3 You must stop. 4 You must look out for children. 5 You must drive slowly. 6 You must turn left.

**Ex 2** 1 You mustn't leave your car here. 2 You mustn't light a cigarette here. 3 You mustn't drive your car here. 4 You mustn't talk to your friends here. 5 You mustn't play football here. 6 You mustn't take your dog for a walk here.

**Ex 3** 1 You mustn't eat sweets. 2 You can eat meat. 3 You can eat vegetables. 4 You mustn't eat cakes. 5 You can eat fish. 6 You mustn't eat chocolate.

## IMPERATIVES

**Ex 1** 1 Turn right. Don't go straight ahead. Don't turn left. 2 Go straight ahead. Don't turn right. Don't turn left. 3 Turn left. Don't go straight ahead. Don't turn right.

**Ex 2** (*all conversations follow the model*)

**Ex 3** 1 Be quiet. Don't talk. 2 Be careful. Don't drop it. 3 Remember to write. Don't forget. 4 Keep still. Don't move. 5 Phone the police. Don't move him. 6 Hurry up. Don't walk so slowly.

**Ex 4** (*student's own answers*)

## INDIRECT OBJECT

**Ex 1** 1 Send her a toy. 2 Buy them a record. 3 Give him a clock. 4 Take her some flowers. 5 Send her a bottle of perfume. 6 Give them a box of chocolates.

**Ex 2** (*student's own answers*: Please bring (*pronoun*) a (*noun*).)

## LET'S

**Ex 1** 1 Yes, let's go to Palm Beach. 2 Well, let's go to the cafe. 3 All right, let's take lemonade and coffee. 4 Yes, let's make some cheese sandwiches. 5 No, let's leave at half past eleven. 6 Yes, let's take apples and oranges.

**Ex 2** (*student's own answers*)

## SIMPLE PRESENT

**Ex 1** 1 likes apples and bananas. 2 like apples and oranges. 3 likes oranges and bananas. 4 likes apples. 5 like apples. 6 like oranges. 7 like bananas.

**Ex 2** 1 Does Mrs Green like oranges? 2 Do Penny and Jenny like apples? 3 Does Don like apples? 4 Does Mr Green like bananas? 5 Do Don and Mrs Green like bananas? 6 Does Mr Green like oranges?

**Ex 3** 1 What 2 Do 3 What 4 Does 5 Do 6 What

**Ex 4** 1 Mr Green likes apples, but he doesn't like oranges. 2 The girls like oranges, but they don't like bananas. 3 Don likes bananas, but he doesn't like apples. 4 Mrs Green likes bananas, but she doesn't like oranges. 5 Mr and Mrs Green like apples, but they don't like oranges. 6 Don likes bananas, but the girls don't like them. 7 The children like oranges, but their parents don't like them.

**Ex 5** (*student's own answers*)

**Ex 6** 1 He's a teacher. He teaches. 2 She's a singer. She sings. 3 He's a writer. He writes. 4 He's a painter. He paints. 5 He's an actor. He acts. 6 She's a dancer. She dances.

## ADVERBS OF FREQUENCY

**Ex 1** 1 He always eats at 12.30. 2 He often works in the garden on Sunday. 3 He sometimes washes the car on Sunday morning. 4 They usually play tennis on Saturday afternoon. 5 he never goes to his office on Saturday. 6 She always visits her mother on Tuesday. 7 He often plays football at school on Tuesday morning. 8 he never watches television . . . . school, . . .

**Ex 2** (*student's own answers*)

**Ex 3** 1 Mr Green shaves every morning. 2 Mrs Green visits her mother every Tuesday. 3 Don dreams about football every night. 4 They have a holiday in France every year. 5 They have turkey and plum pudding every Christmas.

**Ex 4** 1 Mrs Green visits her mother once a week. 2 The girls play tennis twice a week. 3 Mr Green goes to London twice a month. 4 Jenny and Penny brush their teeth three times a day. 5 But they only brush their hair once a day!

**Ex 5** (*student's own answers*)

**Ex 6** 1 He is always busy. 2 His waiting room is never empty. 3 There are usually a lot of people in the morning. 4 There are sometimes a lot of people in the evening, too. 5 Patrick is always there at 6 pm. 6 He is often there at ten o'clock, too. 7 He is always very tired. 8 He is usually asleep at eleven o'clock.

**Ex 7** 1 works 2 likes 3 help 4 are playing 5 play 6 doesn't like 7 likes 8 isn't playing 9 is washing 10 washes 11 wants 12 watches 13 doesn't like

## GOING TO

**Ex 1** I'm going to be + 1 a doctor. 2 a dancer. 3 a footballer. 4 a teacher. 5 a photographer. 6 a racing driver.

**Ex 2** 1 No, Betty is going to take pictures. 2 No, Colin is going to work in a school. 3 No, Fred is going to win races. 4 No, Don is going to play football. 5 No, Jenny is going to help sick people. 6 No, Penny is going to work in a theatre.

**Ex 3** 1 Is Anna going to write a letter? Is she going to do her homework? Is she going to draw a picture? 2 Is Tom going to wash the windows? Is he going to paint the walls? Is he going to mend the roof? 3 Are the girls going to play tennis? Are they going to have a picnic? Are they going to go shopping?

**Ex 4** 1 Anna is going to draw a picture. She isn't going to do her homework. She isn't going to write a letter. 2 Tom isn't going to wash the windows. He isn't going to mend the roof. He's going to paint the walls. 3 The girls aren't going to have a picnic. They aren't going to go shopping. They're going to play tennis.

**Ex 5** (*student's own answers*)

**Ex 6** 1 asks, asking; plays, playing; shows, showing 2 comes, coming; likes, liking; lives, living 3 catches, catching; washes, washing 4 runs, running; begins, beginning 5 flies, flying; hurries, hurrying 6 is washing, washes, to wash 7 runs, is running, to run 8 flies, is flying, to fly

## WAS/WERE

**Ex 1** 1 Yesterday they were at school, too. 2 Yesterday he was at school, too. 3 Yesterday he was in his office, too. 4 Yesterday she was there, too. 5 Yesterday there were two people in the room, too. 6 Yesterday he was out, too. 7 Yesterday they were at home, too. 8 Yesterday there was a bird at the window, too.

**Ex 2** 1 Were Jenny and Penny at school on Monday? 2 Was Don at home on Sunday? 3 Was the manager in his office on Friday? 4 Were there a lot of people at the tennis club on Sunday? 5 Was the baby in the kitchen at eleven o'clock? 6 Was there a letter for Jenny this morning? 7 Were there any letters for Mr Green today?

**Ex 3** 1 he wasn't at work yesterday. 2 they weren't at school yesterday. 3 she wasn't at the supermarket yesterday. 4 there weren't three people at the tennis club yesterday. 5 he wasn't at the cinema yesterday. 6 they weren't in the park yesterday.

**Ex 4** (*student's own answers*)

## HAD

**Ex 1** 1 No, she didn't have it at school. She had it at a friend's house. 2 No, he had it in his office. He didn't have it in a restaurant. 3 No, she had it in a restaurant. She didn't have it at her mother's house. 4 No, he had it at school. He didn't have it at home.

**Ex 2** 1 Did you have lunch at home, Jenny? No, I didn't. 2 Did you have lunch in your/the office, Mr Green? Yes, I did. 3 Did you have lunch at home, Mrs Green? No, I didn't. 4 Where did you have lunch, Mrs Green? In a restaurant. 5 Did you have lunch at home, Don? No, I didn't. 6 Where did you have lunch, Don? At school.

## SIMPLE PAST

**Ex 1** 1 They camped last year. 2 Mr Green/He packed the car last year. 3 The children/They helped him last year. 4 Mrs Green/She baked a cake last year. 5 Mr Green/He looked tired last year. 6 He wanted a cup of tea last year!

**Ex 2** 1 They went to France. 2 They left early in the morning. 3 They took a big tent. 4 Mrs Green bought a lot of food. 5 The children took some toys. 6 They found a good camp site. 7 Everyone went in the sea. 8 They all had a good time.

**Ex 3** 1 She didn't learn to swim last year. 2 He didn't catch a lot of fish last year. 3 They didn't sleep in a small tent last year. 4 They didn't speak French last year. 5 They didn't eat in the restaurant last year. 6 He didn't go with them last year.

**Ex 4** 1 Did Jenny and Penny like the food? 2 Did Mr Green go fishing? 3 Did Don help with the tent? 4 Did the girls swim every day? 5 Did Mrs Green drive the car?

## PREPOSITIONS (PLACE) – SUMMARY

**Ex 1** 1 at 2 out of 3 in 4 to 5 out of 6 to 7 into 8 in 9 to

**Ex 2** 1 D 2 B 3 E 4 C 5 A 6 F

# CARDINAL NUMBERS

## 4 Write these numbers in figures

| 10 | 100 | 1000 | 10000 |
|---|---|---|---|
| ten | a hundred | a thousand | ten thousand |

1 three thousand one hundred and eighty-seven
2 two thousand two hundred and thirty-two
3 three hundred and fifty-two
4 nine thousand four hundred and sixty-eight
5 one thousand five hundred and forty-one
6 six hundred and sixty-nine
7 four thousand seven hundred and seventy-three

| | | | |
|---|---|---|---|
| *3* | *1* | *8* | *7* |
| | | | |
| | | | |
| | | | |
| | | | |
| | | | |
| | | | |

**Now add them.**
**Write your answer in words**

8 ______________________________

**Look at the bottom of the page. Is your answer right?**

## 5 How old are they? Finish the number words

| 13 | 14 | 15 | 16 | 17 | 18 |
|---|---|---|---|---|---|
| 30 | 40 | 50 | 60 | 70 | 80 |

1  

The man is ei *ghty.*

The boy is ei ______

2 

The girl is fi ______

Her mother is fi ______

3 

The woman is fo ______

The boy is fo ______

4 

The man is se ______

His grandson is se ______

5 

The teacher is thi ______

The student is thi ______

6 

The girl is si ______

Her uncle is si ______

ANSWER twenty-two thousand two hundred and twenty-two

# ORDINAL NUMBERS

| 1st | 2nd | 3rd | 4th | 5th | 6th | 7th | 8th | 9th | 10th |
|---|---|---|---|---|---|---|---|---|---|
| first | second | third | fourth | fifth | sixth | seventh | eighth | ninth | tenth |

## 6 Right or wrong?

A B C D E F G H I J K L M N O P Q R S T U V W X Y Z

1 A is the first letter of the alphabet. ✓

2 F is the fifth letter. ×

3 K is the third letter after H. ______

4 D is the third letter before H. ______

5 Y is the second last letter. ______

6 M is the fourteenth letter. ______

7 N is the fourteenth letter. ______

8 T is the twentieth letter. ______

9 Z is the last letter. ______

## 7 Write about these letters

1 A is the *first* letter of the alphabet.

2 B is the ______ letter.

3 D ______

4 H ______

5 L ______

6 O ______

7 R ______

8 V ______

9 Z ______, and it's the last letter, too.

## 8 Finish these sentences

There are 1 *twelve* months in the year. The 2 *first* month is January, and the 3 ______ and last month is December. 4 ______ months have thirty-one days, and four months have 5 ______ days. February, the 6 ______ month, has twenty-eight or twenty-nine days. There are 7 ______ weeks in a year, and 8 ______ days in a week.

## TELLING THE TIME

| four o'clock | ten past four | (a) quarter past four |
|---|---|---|
| half past four | twenty to five | (a) quarter to five |

## 9 What time is it?

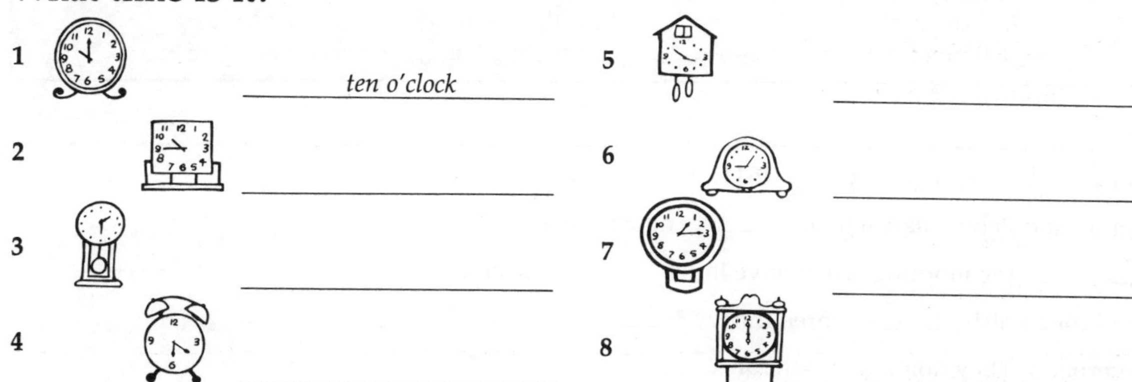

1 *ten o'clock*

2 ____________

3 ____________

4 ____________

5 ____________

6 ____________

7 ____________

8 ____________

| Sometimes we only say numbers | | |
|---|---|---|
| four thirty | eleven forty-five | six twenty-two |

## 10 What time is it?

1 *one fifteen*

2 ____________

3 ____________

4 ____________

5 ____________

6 ____________

7 ____________

8 ____________

# PREPOSITIONS WITH TIME PHRASES

| | | |
|---|---|---|
| AT | (a time)<br>(a festival) | at ten o'clock, at six thirty<br>at Christmas, at Easter<br>NOTE at night |
| ON | (a day)<br>(a date) | on Monday, on my birthday<br>on the first of May, on the tenth of June |
| IN | (a year)<br>(a month)<br>(a century)<br>(a season)<br>(a time of day) | in 1980, in 1815<br>in May, in November<br>in the twentieth century<br>in (the) summer, in (the) winter<br>in the morning, afternoon, evening |

## 1 Write the correct preposition

Jenny and Penny start school 1 ______ nine o'clock 2 ______ the morning. They have lunch 3 ______ twelve, and they finish 4 ______ three thirty 5 ______ afternoon. They don't go to school 6 ______ Saturday or 7 ______ Sunday. Their summer holidays start 8 ______ July and finish 9 ______ September. And they have two or three weeks' holiday 10 ______ Easter and Christmas.

## 2 Look and write

| | |
|---|---|
| **Time of birth** | 9.30 |
| **Morning/afternoon/evening** | Morning |
| **Day** | Saturday |
| **Date** | 9th |
| **Month** | September |
| **Year** | . . . |

She was born *at nine thirty in the morning on Saturday the ninth of September, nineteen* . . .

**Now write a sentence about yourself**

I was born ______________________________

______________________________

# CAN

## CAN (ABILITY)

### 1 Can they? Can't they?

| | | |
|---|---|---|
| Horses<br>Dogs<br>People<br>Lions<br>Monkeys<br>Babies | can<br>can't<br>(= cannot) | drink milk.<br>fly.<br>climb trees.<br>drive cars.<br>eat people.<br>breathe under water.<br>sing songs.<br>carry things. |

**Write true sentences with *can***

Horses ______________________________

Lions ______________________________

Babies ______________________________

Monkeys ______________________________

Dogs ______________________________

People ______________________________

**Now write true sentences with *can't***

People ______________________________

Dogs ______________________________

Lions ______________________________

Babies ______________________________

Monkeys ______________________________

Horses ______________________________

### 2 What about you? And your friend?

Can you swim? play tennis? drive a car? cook? type? play football?
ride a bicycle? . . . .?

I can ______________________ . My friend can ______________________ .

I can't ______________________ . My friend can't ______________________ .

I can ______________________ , but my friend can't ______________________ .

My friend can ______________________ , but I can't ______________________ .

## 3 Look and finish the sentences

1 *They can* climb this tree,
*but they can't climb* that one.

2 ________ carry this boat,
______________________________

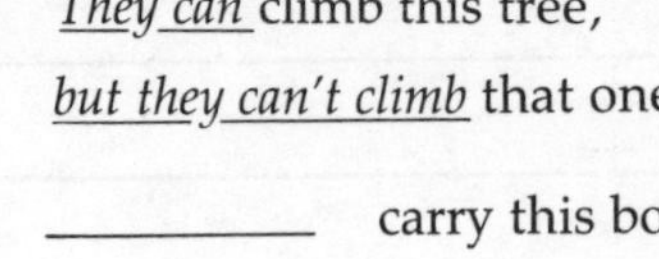

3 ________ ride this bicycle,
______________________________

4 ______ clean this window,
______________________________

5 I ________ post this letter,
______________________________

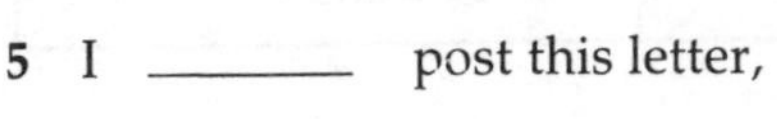

6 ________ carry this case,
______________________________

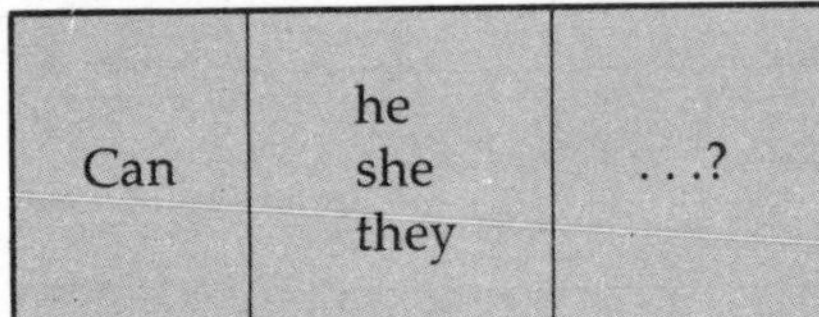

## 4 Ask and answer

| Can | he<br>she<br>they | . . .? |
|---|---|---|

| Yes, | he<br>she<br>they | can. |
|---|---|---|
| No, | | can't. |

1 Don/take good photographs — *Can Don take good photographs?*
*No, he can't.*

2 the baby/drive the car ______________________
______________________

3 the girls/play tennis ______________________
______________________

4 they/play football ______________________
______________________

5 Mr Green/cook ______________________
______________________

## CAN (PERMISSION)

## 5 Write the correct sentences

| Can | we have<br>I borrow<br>we watch<br>we go<br>I play<br>I have | to the cinema?<br>a picnic?<br>a new dress?<br>football?<br>television?<br>your book? |
|---|---|---|

1 Penny: *Can I borrow your book?*

Jenny: No, I need it, sorry.

2 Jenny and Penny: ____________________

Mrs Green: No, it's time for bed now.

3 Don: ____________________

Mr Green: Yes, all right, Don.

4 Jenny: ____________________

Mrs Green: For the party? Yes.

5 Jenny and Penny: ____________________

Mr Green: Maybe. Is it a good film?

6 Don: ____________________

Mrs Green: Yes, if it's good weather.

## 6 Can you or can't you? Finish the sentences

1 *You can* park your car here. __________ park it here.

2 ________ park a motor cycle. ________ park it here.

3 ________ turn right. ________ turn right here.

4 ________ drive fast here. ________ drive fast here.

## 7 What can you do in your English class?

| | | |
|---|---|---|
| speak English? | drink coffee? | play football? |
| sing songs? | talk French? | read books? |
| eat cakes? | draw pictures? | watch television? |
| buy things? | write stories? | ......? |

**Write sentences with *can* and *can't***

We can ____________________

____________________

____________________

____________________

We can't ____________________

____________________

____________________

____________________

## 8 Can you do these things at home?

watch television till midnight?

borrow your father's car?

leave your books in the living room?

spend all your money on ice cream?

**Who says no? Who says yes? Your mother? Your father? Write sentences like this**

> My mother says I can't buy a new dress every week.
> My father says I can't play football after 9 o'clock.

____________________

____________________

____________________

____________________

# MUST

## 1 What must you do?

| You must | stop.<br>turn right/left.<br>be careful.<br>drive slowly.<br>look out for children. |
|---|---|

1 *You must turn right.*
2 ______
3 STOP ______
4 ______
5 30 ______
6 ______

## 2 Find the right answer

| You mustn't | drive<br>leave<br>light<br>play<br>take<br>talk | a cigarette<br>your dog for a walk<br>your car<br>your car<br>to your friends<br>football | here. |
|---|---|---|---|

NO PARKING
NO ENTRY
NO BALL GAMES
NO SMOKING
SILENCE PLEASE
NO DOGS

1 *You mustn't leave your car here.*
2 ______
3 ______
4 ______
5 ______
6 ______

## 3 What does the doctor say?

1 sweets *You mustn't eat sweets.*
2 meat ______
3 vegetables ______
4 cakes ______
5 fish ______
6 chocolate ______

Frances Black is very fat. The doctor says 'You mustn't eat ice cream. You can eat fruit.'

# IMPERATIVES

## 1

| Turn<br>Don't turn | right.<br>left. |
|---|---|
| Go<br>Don't go | straight ahead. |

Turn left. Go straight ahead. Turn right.

**Write three sentences for the pictures**

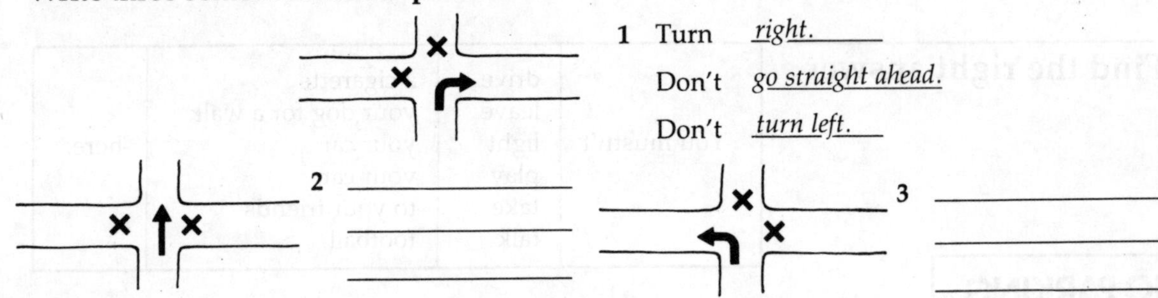

1 Turn *right.*
Don't *go straight ahead.*
Don't *turn left.*

2 ______

3 ______

## 2 Write conversations, like this

| | |
|---|---|
| MRS GREEN: | Remember to buy some bread, please. |
| MR GREEN: | Where? At the supermarket? |
| MRS GREEN: | No, don't go to the supermarket, go to the baker's. |

1 (cheese/grocer's?/supermarket)

MRS GREEN: ______

MR GREEN: ______

MRS GREEN: ______

2 (coffee/supermarket?/grocer's)

YOUR FRIEND: ______

YOU: ______

YOUR FRIEND: ______

3 (fruit/supermarket?/fruit shop)

JENNY: ______

DON: ______

JENNY: ______

# 3 Write two orders for each picture

| Remember to write. |
| --- |
| Hurry up. |
| Keep still. |
| Be quiet. |
| Phone the police. |
| Be careful. |

| | |
| --- | --- |
| (Don't) | drop it.<br>talk.<br>move him.<br>move.<br>walk so slowly.<br>forget. |

1 Shhh!

*Be quiet.*

*Don't talk.*

2 It isn't mine.

________________

________________

3 Goodbye!

________________

________________

4 Put your hands up!

________________

________________

5 An accident!

________________

________________

6 We're late!

________________

________________

# 4 Who says these things to you?

Be quiet! Sit down and open your books. ________________

Please come and help me in the kitchen. ________________

Don't put your coat on the floor. ________________

Don't play your records so loudly! ________________

Come and see me again soon. ________________

# INDIRECT OBJECT

| Give<br>Send<br>Take<br>Buy | him<br>her<br>them | a . . .<br>some . . . |
|---|---|---|

## 1 Write Pat's answers

**1** YOU: What can I send Betty? She has a new baby.

PAT: *Send her a toy.*

**2** YOU: And what can I buy the twins? It's their birthday on Tuesday.

PAT: ______________________________

**3** YOU: What can I give John? He's always late.

PAT: ______________________________

**4** YOU: What can I take Anna? She's in hospital.

PAT: ______________________________

**5** YOU: And what can I send Grandmother for Christmas?

PAT: ______________________________

**6** YOU: What can I give Harry and Kate?

PAT: ______________________________

YOU: Good. Thanks for your help, Pat.

## 2 What do you write?

This is a lotter from your Uncle Bob in New York.

I'm coming to visit you at Christmas. Please write and tell me what everyone wants – you, your parents, your mother and sisters, the baby, everyone!

What do *you* want? Please bring *me* a ______________________________

Your mother? Please bring ______________________________

Your father? Please ______________________________

Your brothers/sisters? ______________________________

# LET'S

## 1 Complete the conversation: write sentences with *let's* and the words in brackets

| Let's | go to . . .<br>have lunch at . . .<br>take . . . |
|---|---|

1 JIM: What can we do today? Go to the beach?
DOT: That's a good idea. Yes, (Palm Beach)

*Yes, let's go to Palm Beach.*

2 JIM: What about lunch? There's a restaurant and a cafe, I think.
DOT: Well, (the cafe)

_______________

3 JIM: But take something to drink, too, please.
DOT: All right, (lemonade and coffee)

_______________

4 JIM: And I'm always hungry at the beach. Can we make some sandwiches?
DOT: Yes, (some cheese sandwiches)

_______________

5 JIM: When can we leave? Now?
DOT: No, (at half past eleven)

_______________

6 JIM: And can we take some fruit?
DOT: Yes, (apples and oranges)

_______________

JIM: Good! I'm always *very* hungry at the beach!

## 2 What do you think? Answer with *Let's . . .*

We can have fish or meat or chicken for lunch. _______________

We can go out for a meal, or have dinner at home. _______________

We can watch television or go to the cinema tonight. _______________

We can play tennis or football or go for a walk now. _______________

This summer we can go camping or stay in a hotel. _______________

And we can go to the sea or the mountains. _______________

# SIMPLE PRESENT

## 1 What do they like?

| I<br>You<br>We<br>They | like . . . |
|---|---|

| He<br>She | likes . . . |
|---|---|

| | apples | oranges | bananas |
|---|---|---|---|
| Mr Green | yes | | |
| Mrs Green | yes | | yes |
| Penny<br>Jenny | yes | yes | |
| Don | | yes | yes |

**Complete these sentences**

1 Mrs Green *likes apples* and *bananas*.

2 Penny and Jenny __________ and __________

3 Don __________ and __________

4 Mr Green __________

5 Mrs Green and the girls __________

6 Don and the girls __________

7 Mrs Green and Don __________

## 2 Ask questions

| Do | I<br>you<br>we<br>they | like . . .? |
|---|---|---|

| Does | he<br>she | like . . .? |
|---|---|---|

1 Mrs Green/oranges *Does Mrs Green like oranges?*

2 Penny and Jenny/apples __________

3 Don/apples __________

4 Mr Green/bananas __________

5 Don and Mrs Green/bananas __________

6 Mr Green/oranges __________

# 3 Look at the answers and complete the questions with *What, Do/Does*

| What does Don like? | Oranges and bananas. |
|---|---|
| Do the girls like apples? | Yes, they do. |

1 *What* does Mrs Green like? — Apples and bananas.
2 ______ Penny and Jenny like bananas? — No, they don't.
3 ______ does Don like? — Oranges and bananas.
4 ______ Mr Green like oranges? — No, he doesn't.
5 ______ Don and the girls like them? — Yes, they do.
6 ______ doesn't Don like? — Apples.

# 4 What don't they like?

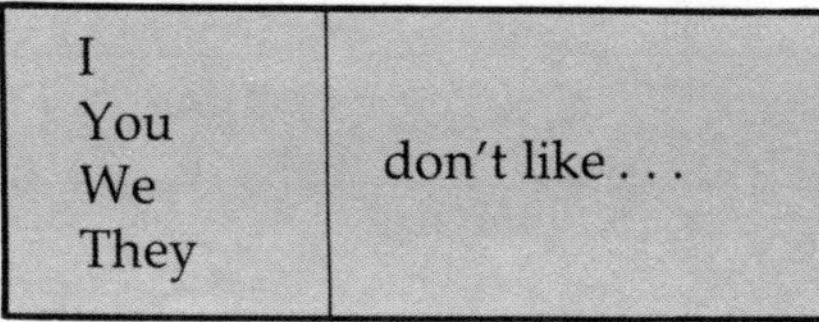

| I<br>You<br>We<br>They | don't like . . . |
|---|---|

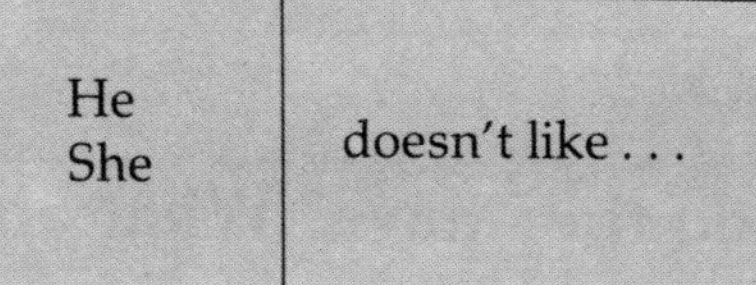

| He<br>She | doesn't like . . . |
|---|---|

**Write sentences**

1 Mr Green/apples/oranges

*Mr Green likes apples but he doesn't like oranges.*

2 The girls/oranges/bananas

______________________________

3 Don/bananas/apples

______________________________

4 Mrs Green/bananas/oranges

______________________________

5 Mr and Mrs Green/apples/oranges

______________________________

6 Don/bananas/the girls/them

______________________________

7 The children/oranges/their parents/them

______________________________

## 5 What about you?

Do you like apples? oranges? bananas? ice cream? chocolate? cakes? lemonade? Coca Cola? tea? coffee?

**What do you like?**

I ______________________

______________________

**What don't you like?**

______________________

______________________

**What does your family like?**

We ______________________

______________________

**What don't they like?**

______________________

______________________

**What does your friend like?**

He/She ______________________

______________________

**What doesn't he/she like?**

______________________

______________________

**What do all your friends like?**

They ______________________

______________________

**What don't they like?**

______________________

______________________

## 6 What jobs do they have? What do they do?

**Complete the sentences**

1 He's a teacher.
*He teaches.*

2 ____________ singer.
She ____________

3 He ________ writer.
______________________

4 ____________ painter.
______________________

5 ____________ actor.
______________________

6 ____________ dancer.
______________________

# ADVERBS OF FREQUENCY

| | | | |
|---|---|---|---|
| He<br>She | always<br>usually<br>often<br>sometimes<br>never | goes<br>eats<br>works | . . . |
| They | | visit<br>play | |

## 1 Write sentences

1 It's 12.30. The baby is eating. (always)

*He always eats at 12.30.*

2 It's Sunday. Mr Green is working in the garden. (often) ____________

____________

3 It's Sunday morning. Don is washing the car. (sometimes) ____________

____________

4 It's Saturday afternoon. The girls are playing tennis. (usually) ____________

____________

5 It's Saturday. Mr Green isn't going to his office. (never)

No, ____________

____________

6 It's Tuesday. Mrs Green is visiting her mother. (always)

____________

____________

7 It's Tuesday morning. Don is playing football at school. (often) ____________

____________

8 He isn't watching television. (never)

No, ____________

on Tuesday morning. Why not? Because

he's at ____________

of course!

## 2 Read this

Mr Green often gets up before seven, and he usually has breakfast at seven thirty. He leaves the house at eight, and he always starts work at 8.45. He sometimes eats at twelve and he sometimes eats at one. He usually comes home at six o'clock, and the Greens always have dinner at seven. They often watch television in the evening. Mr Green always watches the news at nine, and he never goes to bed after midnight.

**What about you?**

| I | always<br>usually<br>often<br>sometimes<br>never | get up<br>leave the house<br>eat | at . . . |
|---|---|---|---|

When do you . . .

. . . get up? ______________________

. . . start work/school? ______________________

. . . come home? ______________________

## 3 How often? Find the right sentences

5

| Mrs Green visits her mother<br>Mr Green shaves<br>They have turkey and plum pudding<br>Don dreams about football<br>They have a holiday in France | every Christmas.<br>every night.<br>every year.<br>every Tuesday.<br>every morning. |
|---|---|

1 *Mrs Green visits her mother every Tuesday.*

2 ______________________

3 ______________________

4 ______________________

5 ______________________

4

2

3

1

## 4 How often?

| once<br>twice<br>three times | a | day<br>week<br>month |
|---|---|---|

**Rewrite these sentences**

1 Mrs Green visits her mother every Tuesday.
*Mrs Green visits her mother once a week.*

2 The girls play tennis every Saturday and every Sunday.

3 Mr Green goes to London on the 1st and the 15th of every month.

4 Jenny and Penny brush their teeth after breakfast, lunch and dinner.

5 But they only brush their hair before breakfast!

## 5 What about you? How often do you do these things?

often? never? once/twice/three times a day/week/month/year?

. . . brush your hair?

. . . wash your face?

. . . shave?

. . . see your mother's/father's family?

. . . drink lemonade for breakfast?

. . . watch television?

**And what about your friend?**

My friend often ________

He/She never ________

He/She ________ once a week.

He/She ________ ten times a day!

# 6 Be + Adverbs of Frequency

| | | |
|---|---|---|
| am<br>is<br>are | always<br>often<br>usually<br>sometimes<br>never | busy<br>empty |

## Write sentences

1 Patrick is a doctor. He is busy. (always)

*He is always busy.*

2 His waiting room is empty. (never)

3 There are a lot of people in the morning. (usually)

4 There are a lot of people in the evening, too. (sometimes)

5 Patrick is there at 6 pm. (always)

6 He is there at ten o'clock, too. (often)

7 He is very tired. (always)

8 He is asleep at eleven o'clock. (usually)

# 7 Write the correct form of the verb

Mr Green 1 *works* in an office from Monday to Friday, so he often 2 ______ to (work)(like)
work in the garden on Saturday and Sunday. Sometimes the girls 3 ______ him, (help)
but not today. They 4 ________ tennis now. They usually 5 ________ tennis on (play; play)
Saturday and Sunday. Don 6 ____________________ tennis. He (not like)
7 ________________ football. He 8 ________________ football now, he (like; not play)
9 ________________ the car. He often 10 __________ it on Sunday. (wash; wash)
He 11 ______ to watch a football match on TV at four o'clock. (want)
Mrs Green never 12 ______ football – she 13 ________________ it. (watch) (not like)

# GOING TO

## 1 What are they going to be in the year 2000?

Jenny

Penny

Don

Colin

Betty

Fred

| | | |
|---|---|---|
| dancer | doctor | footballer |
| photographer | racing driver | teacher |

1 Jenny *I'm going to be a doctor.*

2 Penny ______

3 Don ______

4 Colin ______

5 Betty ______

6 Fred ______

## 2 What are they going to do? Look at the pictures again

1 Who is going to take pictures? Penny?
*No, Betty is going to take pictures.*

2 Who is going to work in a school? Don?

______

3 Who is going to win races? Jenny?

______

4 Who is going to play football? Fred?

______

5 Who is going to help sick people? Colin?

______

6 Who is going to work in a theatre? Betty?

______

# 3 What are they going to do? Ask questions

| Is | he/she | going to . . .? |
|---|---|---|
| Are they | | |

1

write a letter
do her homework
draw a picture

*Is Anna going to write a letter?*
*Is she going to do her homework?*
*Is she going to draw a picture?*

2 Is Tom ______________________

Is he ______________________

______________________

wash the windows
paint the walls
mend the roof

3

play tennis
have a picnic
go shopping

_____ the girls ______________________

______________________

______________________

# 4 Now write the answers

1 Anna is *going to draw a picture.*

She isn't *going to do her homework.*

And she *isn't going to write a letter.*

2 Tom *isn't* ______________________

He *isn't* ______________________

______________________

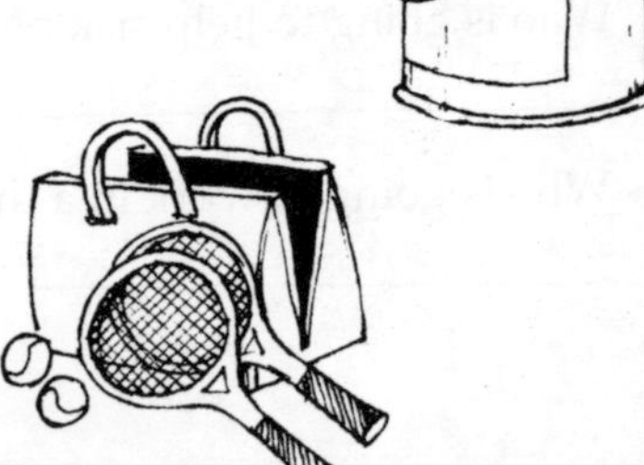

3 The girls _____ n't ______________________

They _____ n't ______________________

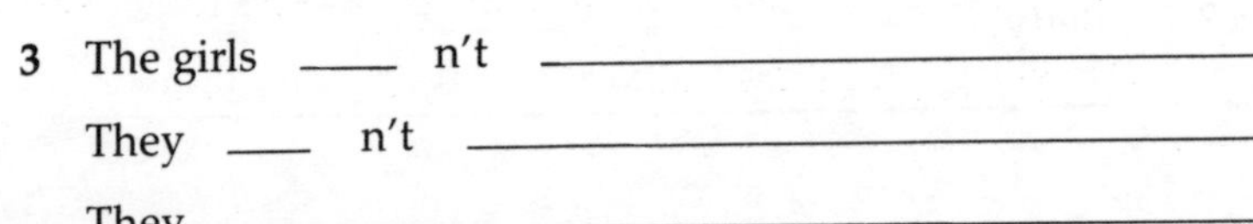

They ______________________

## 5 What are you going to do?

Are you going to draw today? Are you going to paint? Are you going to play tennis?

**Write two things you are going to do today and next week**

Today ______________________________

______________________________

Next week ______________________________

______________________________

## 6 Can you spell these words?

1

| (to) | | ask | play | show |
|---|---|---|---|---|
| (he) | + s | *asks* | | |
| (is) | + ing | *asking* | | |

2

| | come | like | live |
|---|---|---|---|
| + s | | | |
| ~~e~~ + ing | | | |

3

| | catch | wash |
|---|---|---|
| + es | | |
| + ing | | |

4

| | run | begin |
|---|---|---|
| + s | | |
| + (n)ing | | |

5

| | fly | hurry |
|---|---|---|
| ~~y~~ + ies | | |
| + ing | | |

**Now choose the right word for each sentence.**

6 Jenny *is washing* her hair. She __________ it twice a week. She's going __________ it again on Friday.

7 Don __________ to school every day. He's late, so he __________ now. And he's going __________ to school again tomorrow. He's always late!

8 Polly is a stewardess. She __________ every day. She __________ to Paris now. And tomorrow she is going __________ to Cairo.

# WAS/WERE

## 1 Write sentences

| I<br>He<br>She<br>There | was . . . |
|---|---|

| We<br>You<br>They<br>There | were . . . |
|---|---|

1 It's Wednesday. Jenny and Penny are at school.
*Yesterday they were at school, too.*

2 Don is at school.

______________________________

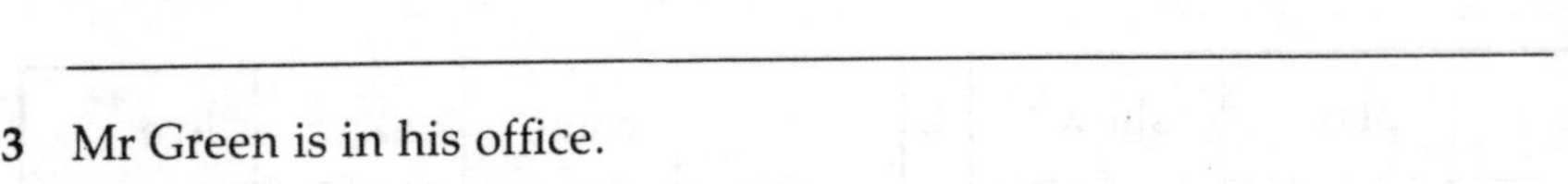

3 Mr Green is in his office.

______________________________

4 His secretary is there.

______________________________

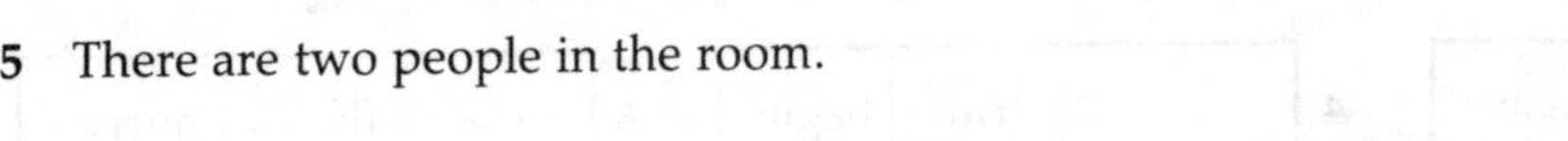

5 There are two people in the room.

______________________________

6 The manager is out.

______________________________

7 Mrs Green and the baby are at home.

______________________________

8 There's a bird at the window.

______________________________

## 2 Ask questions

| Was | he<br>she<br>there | . . .? |
|---|---|---|

| Were | they<br>there | . . .? |
|---|---|---|

1 Jenny and Penny/at school/Monday
*Were Jenny and Penny at school on Monday?*

2 Don/at home/Sunday

______________________________

3 the manager/in his office/Friday

______________________________

4 there/a lot of people/at the tennis club/Sunday

______________________________

5 the baby/kitchen/eleven o'clock

______________________________

6 there/a letter for Jenny/this morning

______________________________

7 there/any letters/Mr Green/today

______________________________

## 3 Finish the sentences

| I<br>He<br>She<br>There | wasn't . . . |
|---|---|

| We<br>You<br>They<br>There | weren't . . . |
|---|---|

1 It's Monday. Mr Green is at work today, but *he wasn't at work yesterday.*

2 The children are at school, but ______________________________

3 Anna is in the supermarket, but ______________________________

4 There are three people at the tennis club, but ______________________________

5 Don is at the cinema, but ______________________________

6 Mrs Green and the baby are in the park, but ______________________________

## 4 What about you? Give short answers

| Yes, | I was.<br>we were.<br>there was.<br>there were. |
|---|---|

| No, | I wasn't.<br>we weren't.<br>there wasn't.<br>there weren't. |
|---|---|

Were you at home all day yesterday? ______________

Were you and your friends at school? ______________

Were there a lot of people with you? ______________

Were you happy? ______________

Were you in bed at midnight? ______________

Was there a good programme on television last night? ______________

# HAD

| I/We<br>You<br>He/She<br>They | had<br><br>didn't have | . . . |
|---|---|---|

## 1 Where did they have lunch yesterday?

|  |  |  |  |
|---|---|---|---|
| Jenny: at a friend's house | Don: at school | Mr Green: in his office | Mrs Green: in a restaurant |

1 Did Jenny have lunch at school? *No, she didn't have it at school.*
*She had it at a friend's house.*

2 Did Mr Green have lunch in a restaurant? ____________

3 Did Mrs Green have lunch at her mother's house? ____________

4 Did Don have lunch at home? ____________

## 2 Ask questions and answer them

| Did you have lunch | at school?<br>at home?<br>at work? | Yes, I did.<br>No, I didn't. |
|---|---|---|
| Where did you have lunch? | | At . . ./In . . . |

1 home/Jenny? *Did you have lunch at home, Jenny?* No, *I didn't.*
2 office/Mr Green? ____________ ____ I did.
3 at home/Mrs Green? ____________ No, ____
4 Where/Mrs Green? ____________ __ a restaurant.
5 home/Don? ____________ ____ didn't.
6 Where/Don? ____________ ____ school.

# SIMPLE PAST

Add (e)d to regular verbs to form the past

## 1 What happened last year? Write sentences

The Greens are going on holiday tomorrow.

1 They always camp.

*They camped last year.*

2 Mr Green is packing the car.

______________________

3 The children are helping him.

______________________

4 Mrs Green is baking a cake.

______________________

5 Mr Green looks tired.

______________________

6 He wants a cup of tea!

______________________

## 2 What did the Greens do last year?

Learn irregular verbs: go/went, leave/left etc.

1 (go to France) *They went to France.*

2 (leave early in the morning) ______________________

3 (take a big tent) ______________________

4 (Mrs Green/buy a lot of food) ______________________

5 (the children/take some toys) ______________________

6 (find a good camp site) ______________________

7 (everyone/go in the sea) ______________________

8 (they all/have a good time) ______________________

## 3 What didn't they do last year?

| He<br>She<br>They | didn't | learn<br>eat<br>speak | . . . |
|---|---|---|---|

1 This year Penny is going to learn to swim.
*She didn't learn to swim last year.*

2 Don is going to catch a lot of fish.
______________________________

3 The children are going to sleep in a small tent.
______________________________

4 They are going to speak French.
______________________________

5 They're going to eat in the restaurant.
______________________________

6 The baby is going to go with them.
______________________________

(Why not? Because he's only eight months old!)

## 4 Ask questions

| Did | you<br>he<br>she<br>they | like<br>swim | . . .? |
|---|---|---|---|

1 Mr and Mrs Green liked the food.
(Jenny and Penny) *Did Jenny and Penny like the food?* Yes, they did.

2 Don went fishing.
(Mr Green) ______________________________ No, he didn't.

3 Penny helped with the tent.
(Don) ______________________________ Yes, he did.

4 Mrs Green swam every day.
(the girls) ______________________________ No, they didn't.

5 Mr Green drove the car.
(Mrs Green) ______________________________ Yes, she did.

# PREPOSITIONS (PLACE) - SUMMARY

| WITH MOVEMENT | | | WITHOUT MOVEMENT | | |
|---|---|---|---|---|---|
| to go<br>to come | to<br>from | London<br>England<br>school<br>work<br>the cinema | to be | in | London<br>England<br>bed<br>hospital |
| to go | into | a room | | at | school<br>work<br>the cinema<br>home |
| to put sth | | a basket | | | |
| to come | out of | a room | | | |
| to take sth | | a basket | | | |

## 1 Find the right prepositions

| at | in | in | into | out of | out of | to | to | to |
|---|---|---|---|---|---|---|---|---|

Jenny and Penny are [1]*at* school. It's two minutes to ten, and they're coming [2]_____ their classroom – they have a gym lesson at ten. Now they're [3]_____ the gymnasium. They're listening to the gym teacher.

'Run [4]_____ the end of the gym. Take a ball [5]_____ the basket. Throw it and catch it. Stop! Bring the balls and the basket back [6]_____ me. Put the balls [7]_____ the basket. Are they all [8]_____ the basket now? Good. Now run [9]_____ the window.'

## 2 Which picture?

1 Jenny is beside the teacher. ___*D*___
2 Penny is on Jenny's back. ______
3 Jenny is behind the teacher. ______
4 Penny is near the window. ______
5 Jenny is in front of Penny. ______
6 The horse is between Jenny and Penny. ______

| WITH MOVEMENT OR WITHOUT MOVEMENT | | |
|---|---|---|
| to put sth<br>to go<br>to be | on<br>under<br>near<br>beside<br>behind<br>in front of | the table<br>the window<br>your friend |
| | between | . . . and . . . |

# LIST OF VERBS

## TO BE

| Affirmative | | Negative | | Question | |
|---|---|---|---|---|---|
| I am | we are | I'm not | we aren't | am I? | are we? |
| you are | | you aren't | | are you? | |
| he is | they are | he isn't | they aren't | is he? | are they? |
| she is | | she isn't | | is she? | |
| it is | | it isn't | | is it? | |
| I was | we were | I wasn't | we weren't | was I? | were we? |
| you were | | you weren't | | were you? | |
| he was | they were | he wasn't | they weren't | was he? | were they? |
| she was | | she wasn't | | was she? | |
| it was | | it wasn't | | was it? | |

## TO HAVE

| Affirmative | | Negative | | Question | |
|---|---|---|---|---|---|
| I have | we have | I don't have | we don't have | do I have? | do we have? |
| you have | | you don't have | | do you have? | |
| he has | they have | he doesn't have | they don't have | does he have? | do they have? |
| she has | | she doesn't have | | does she have? | |
| it has | | it doesn't have | | does it have? | |

| REGULAR VERBS | | | IRREGULAR VERBS | | |
|---|---|---|---|---|---|
| ask | asks | asked | bring | brings | brought |
| camp | camps | camped | buy | buys | bought |
| carry | carries | carried | come | comes | came |
| finish | finishes | finished | do | does | did |
| help | helps | helped | drink | drinks | drank |
| hurry | hurries | hurried | drive | drives | drove |
| like | likes | liked | eat | eats | ate |
| look | looks | looked | find | finds | found |
| play | plays | played | give | gives | gave |
| start | starts | started | go | goes | went |
| stay | stays | stayed | learn | learns | learnt/-ed |
| talk | talks | talked | leave | leaves | left |
| (tele)phone | -phones | -phoned | make | makes | made |
| visit | visits | visited | put | puts | put |
| walk | walks | walked | read | reads | read |
| want | wants | wanted | ride | rides | rode |
| wash | washes | washed | run | runs | ran |
| watch | watches | watched | see | sees | saw |
| work | works | worked | send | sends | sent |
| | | | sing | sings | sang |
| | | | sleep | sleeps | slept |
| | | | take | takes | took |
| | | | tell | tells | told |
| | | | write | writes | wrote |
| | | | can, must (present tense only) | | |

These verbs also occur, but not in all persons/tenses. They are often with a picture and are mainly for passive recognition.

| | | | | | |
|---|---|---|---|---|---|
| act | clean | drop | mend | remember | throw |
| borrow | climb | feed | move | shave | turn |
| breathe | dance | fly | paint | show | type |
| brush | draw | forget | park | spend | win |
| catch | dream | keep | post | teach | |